# Some Other Life

*poems by*

# Tracy Seffers

*Finishing Line Press*
Georgetown, Kentucky

# Some Other Life

Copyright © 2017 by Tracy Seffers
ISBN 978-1-63534-270-3 First Edition
All rights reserved under International and Pan-American Copyright Conventions.
No part of this book may be reproduced in any manner whatsoever without written permission from the publisher, except in the case of brief quotations embodied in critical articles and reviews.

## ACKNOWLEDGMENTS

Some Other Life; Mulberry Shaking, The resurrection, when it comes: in *Backbone Mountain Review*
Hauling Hay: in *Assisi: A Literary Journal*; (with permission) by Southeastern Writers Group in *First Light II*
Lessons in Ballad-Singing: in *Backbone Mountain Review* and (with permission) in the *Appalachian Writer's Anthology* (Frank X Walker); and Finalist, *Still Journal* 2013 Literary Contest (poetry category)
Ruins: in *Pine Mountain Sand & Gravel Literary Journal*
Shenandoah River Sequence (I. Mourning, 2. Noon, 3. River Moon Rising): in the *Appalachian Writers Anthology* (Silas House)
To Know a River: in *Still: A Journal* and (with permission) by Southeastern Writers Group in *First Light II*
Two-Dog Night: in *Still: A Journal*
Understory: in *Still: A Journal* (2012 Literary Contest Judge's Selection for Poetry) and Honorable Mention, 2012 West Virginia Writers Competition for Poetry
Yalad: in the *Bluestone Review*


Publisher: Leah Maines

Editor: Christen Kincaid

Cover Art: Mary W. Cogley

Author Photo: Carolyn Aselton Wilkie

Cover Design: Elizabeth Maines McCleavy


Printed in the USA on acid-free paper.
Order online: www.finishinglinepress.com
also available on amazon.com

Author inquiries and mail orders:
Finishing Line Press
P. O. Box 1626
Georgetown, Kentucky 40324
U. S. A.

# Table of Contents

Some Other Life ............................................................. 1
Shenandoah River Sequence
    I – Morning ...................................................... 2
    II – Noon .......................................................... 3
    III – River Moon Rising ................................. 4
Pierced ............................................................................ 6
A Fine Hand .................................................................. 8
Ruins (in memoriam) .................................................. 9
After We Pray .............................................................. 10
Mulberry Shaking ...................................................... 11
Pomegranates ............................................................. 12
Hauling Hay ................................................................ 14
Two-Dog Night (Insomnia) ..................................... 16
Relinquishment .......................................................... 17
The resurrection, when it comes ........................... 18
Yalad ............................................................................. 20
The Root Defiant (for Katy) ..................................... 21
River Prayers
    I – Eden, Imagined ....................................... 22
    II – All Things Rise ....................................... 23
    III – To Know a River .................................. 24
    IV – Messenger ............................................. 26
Lessons in Ballad-Singing ....................................... 27
Understory (Red in the Bud) .................................. 28

**Some Other Life**

Things fall away: the parent, the late-grown child,
the shabby green cloak of late summer,
mountains, and the dreams of mountains.

What remains: the bones of things laid bare,
stark sycamore-white limbs of trees,
the ridgeline breathing deeply, the river beneath;

and beneath it all, all that has fallen down,
fallen away, heaped up in the sweet decay
of winter, some other life begins to flow.

# SHENANDOAH RIVER SEQUENCE

I
Morning

Trailing bitterness, I descend our hill, clumsily splashing coffee
on Shenandoah's bank, my morning libation to the river god
before setting out. The sun has not yet blinked awake;
mist sleeps still on the river's face. This is the time of blessing:
sacred silence before the world growls into motion.

Grandfather sycamore stands, naked yet courteous,
old friend and flowing river's faithful sentinel.
In time, he knows, her waters will take him too,
to rest beside his silent siblings in their river grave.
Wet roots tangle like memories, dark lace glowing in half-light.

On the water now, I glide past them in silent lines along the banks;
they rest, starkly white against the darker trees.
Sycamores grow near streams, my father taught me,
where their bright flesh, even on moonless nights,
will mark flowing water, the way to freedom.
Moss grows to the north; there's your path.

Stroke, and turn: the grandfather stands, his limbs
broken and branching, pale lightning in the dim air.
Old Charlie, the resident black snake as thick as my arm,
inches imperceptibly, improbably up the straight bare trunk,
to drape himself companionably where the earliest light will warm.
I dip my paddle, set off for home.

II
Noon

River wears her bones deep.
I float, glass-still water mirroring parallax worlds:
paddle dripping ripples into silent sky, ridge, trees, shoreline
suspended; river clings to river, shoreline, trees, ridge,
and endless, silver sky. In the dappled hush,
grey heron, disturbed, beat heavily skyward,
bodies lifting silently from the water, lifting as they go
something heavy within me—that droning engine—
and I am released into a wordless sufficiency.

Through the cupped hands of her banks flows a world:
water and land and sky—
sky above, sky below, dizzy with sky I drift.

A sudden limestone ridge
swims up through murky river-sky
and anchors me, surprises me to earth again,
a rocky spine along her slender back.

*River*, I say. *River*,

*Like you, I am both earth and water, both sky and stone.*
*I long to roll my spine against yours, match us*
*bone to bone. Here could I sleep, drifting*
*weightless, wordless, worldless.*

III
River Moon Rising

*Amazing grace, how sweet the sound that saved*

You are flowing away from me, there in your bed, your river bed.
Moon tangles in a net of trees above the ridge, shimmering
like my pale fingers through the black swirl
of my mother's abandoned hair.
In winter, your icy waters run an unnamable blue-gray-green,
quiet river blood in my mother's patient veins.
Her hands were not this cold,
not yet, not yet,
when I sat beside her bed and held them,
when I finally sang to her at the black river's edge.

*A wretch like me I once was lost but*


I had no songs for her before. The regret of years has turned
to bitter water in my mouth, now when no song can call her back.
Even so, even so:
I sang beside her bed, I sang to bind my own heart, I sang
forgiveness.

Did you hear me, in the silence hidden behind your eyes?

*Now am found was blind but now*

Old grandfather sycamore glows in the moonlight,
shocking pale as her skin, smooth and lovely as a young girl's,
despite, despite.

*I see.*

These were your gifts:
to gather with my sisters
to bathe you in silence
to see your final beauty when all else had turned to ashes
to sing you home, still singing as the bitter river rose,
flowing into moonlight.

**Pierced**

At your funeral, we dissolved into
helpless giggles, mortifying
our families, ruffling the priest;
but we couldn't stop
the memory that came unbidden—

my sister and I, trying so hard to be
good daughters, trying so hard to be
of use, to do *something* (nothing to be done,
says the doctor) as you lay couch-bound
(before you were bedridden)—

fetching, fussing, cooking, rubbing
your poor cold crusty feet
until you asked us to stop,
*stop please*, and let you rest.

Somehow, cleaning the old alpine cuckoo clock
hanging dusty in the hallway seemed
like a good idea.   Until, that is,
it detached, slipped from hands
shaky with grief, launched itself
at my sister's head, hurtling with its ornate
regal carved buck's head and full rack
to break apart against her broad forehead.
She stood stunned (deer in the headlights)—
I stood stunned watching one broken antler
quiver, standing straight out from her brow
where it had struck, and stuck—
our good and hopeful deed punished.

As blood began to pool and trickle down
her astonished face, we came back to life
and packed sister and deer and clock-shards
down the hallway for repairs. I can't remember
if we were laughing or crying.

What I remember is this:
Your small fist raised, threatening thunder,
whispering: *Such a klop!* Brief smile.
Released then, we fell about the room, hooting.

Such relief, that laughter—such a relief to be pierced
by something other than the hard, pointed fact
of your leaving us behind
with all our broken clocks.

**A Fine Hand**

Out of the corner of my eye, I saw: slight tremor, fork wavering
In a breeze it alone felt. I saw then, too, my hand, a replica of my mother's:
Long ridged thumbnail, ropey veins, crazed networks of wrinkles,
A lifetime already of dishwashing, list-writing and pie crusts. No regrets.

Beneath lunchtime chat and laughter, political rages, old sweet jokes,
Another voice I alone heard: my mother cocked a dubious brow
At my fork: "*Nu?* You'd want to get that checked out. It's probably nothing.
But if—well, you'd want to get it right." Even from beyond, where dance

Her red heels, where her wild head-thrown-back laughter bothers no one,
She is reaching back to elbow my rib, pinch my soft underarm. Still mama.
Still mama in her chair, the last time she'd sit there, struggling to maintain
Her fine, tremulous hand to make one final list for Dad. That night,

Hospice would arrive, ointments and papers, gentle, pointed conversation.
We'd help her to the table, she would sign her name with a flourish,
The DNR order that said *I am ready. Let me go.* Later, I found that list—
Just her signature over and over. You'd want to get it right. No regrets.

**Ruins**
>   *(in memoriam)*


This house's angles have been sagging off-square, its walls mourning
toward the tangle of the horizon, for some years now,
long before the fire that tried, but failed, to bring it down.

It still stands, though now a tree has fallen—when I do not know—
and has shouldered an old screen porch aside.  How many times
have I passed this spot and failed to see, failed to imagine

what this house must have been like when loved, bright flags
of laundry above the dusty skates, Big Wheels and dog dishes,
breeze chiming calm over the swing where eave songs hummed?

I am surprised by the tenderness I feel for empty places:
this house wearing its scars, broken stones of a solitary chimney,
a well that eases no child's thirst.  Ruined for years,

perhaps it was wisdom to wait for the slow unfolding
of winter into spring, the incremental greening
of these grey angles, all my empty lines and spaces.

Fire burns, tree falls.  Still standing.

**After We Pray**

Find the children. Are they hungry, are they cold? Feed them.
Make the pot of soup, the stack of pancakes, biscuits and gravy.
Hot cocoa, sweet milk, a second mug, a third.
This is what we do.

Find the survivors. Are they hurt, broken, in need of mending?
Stitch them, carry them, cover them with your own tattered coat.
Stand with them as the flames eat what remains. Open your arms.
This is what we do.

Find the one who mourns. Sit. Hold the hand. Remain silent.
Weep and weep again, until your tears and theirs run together,
a river, an ocean soaking into earth parched and broken by war.
This is what we do.

Stand with those who gather against the darkness.
Bring the wood for the fire that warms them.
Raise your fist alongside. Rage for justice.
Change this world, change your heart,
change what we can reach.

Weep, sigh, rage, change.
This too is prayer.
This is what we do.

## Mulberry Shaking

It was useful then to be small, the smallest of our seven,
back in midsummer when mulberries ripened, each
a purple-black thumbprint against the wide green leaf.

My brother and I—incorrigible climbers we were—
scampered up into the mulberry's arms,
our mother peering up at us with one hand propped on her hip,

the other shading her eyes. She turned then and handed
a stack of berry sheets to our older sisters, and began their work—
spreading the gloriously blotched sheets beneath the tree,

close around the trunk, lapping edge over edge, spreading
sheet after sheet all the way out to the edge of shadow,
the furthest reaches of its canopy, and beyond.

A glance around to see that the bowls were ready, then a signal—
the cue to begin our dance. Standing and gripping branches overhead,
we dipped at the knees, pushing and shaking each limb—gently at first,

then with greater confidence as we sensed the tree's response.
Berries pattered below on the sheets—gently at first, then
a steady rain. The command to stop, as our sisters' bowls had filled

to overflowing, became time to stop and eat a few ourselves. The dance
continued until the rain slowed and mother satisfied. My brother
was off, then, to find his place. But I would always linger

there in the cool arms of the tree, brushed by the breeze always stirring,
languidly plucking another berry here, another there, sucking my fingers,
thinking with pleasure of the pies and cobblers to come; and the invitation

there, too, to help her in the kitchen: dusting the board with flour,
measuring and sifting carefully—these even my small hands could do,
as important, really, as the dance that shook all the sweetness down.

**Pomegranates**

It taunted me, the original tree of temptation, as I passed
the sagging fence each morning on my walk to school.
It grew with me, each year taller, fuller, laden branches reaching

beyond the rusted links as though inviting me. I knew it was wrong,
knew that reaching back to take the proffered fruit, heavy and warm,
would be my own Eden to lose, or to gain. Yet one morning,

desire for the imagined sweet beneath the dappled leather
would not be restrained. My hand found the nearest fruit
hanging outside the fence—grasped, twisted; and it was mine.

                                      Not yet, not yet—

the work of desire was still ahead, to rend that flesh, discover
the delicate membranes pitted and coiled with rubies, aflame
in the early Texas sun, fed by the same black volcanic soil

that grimed feet and nails all summer, grew its stubborn harvests.
Such a struggle, that feast—the rind tough and resistant, the tiny seeds
reluctant to the last. The taste, sharp and acid, surprised my tongue,

setting it alight, waking unexpected hunger,
for what I could not say. Not then.
These days, the task is cleaner,

no theft involved, just the choosing when the store heaps them up
as now, in winter, a sign of summer's breathing elsewhere for a while.
Even the work of seeding is easier, since a sister taught me how,

filling a bowl with clear cold water, holding the fruit under the surface
to break open the ruddy skin, let the pith and membranes split and float,
the secret seeds release and sink, a layer of patient jewels;

waiting even so to prod my memory, some forty years later,
with their bitter and their sweet, their startled-awake clarity;
their taste of longing, of every dusty summer in my mouth.

## Hauling Hay

The summer sun blazed, but farmers think at least two seasons ahead:
winter was on your mind, when the cows follow in steam, bellowing,
looking to you for forage. The boys had already left home, launching
out from our small farm, to find their own way. Mom and I alone

were left behind to be your helpers; though we weren't much help,
and more often you just worked longer, bending your brown back
to the extra chores. But it was time to bring in hay bales for winter;
strong as you were, you couldn't haul it alone. At fifteen, I was it.

So before sunrise, while it was still cool, you drove us
to a local hayfield in your orange Dodge, homemade hay rack
reaching up from the top of the bed, measuring high the work ahead.
Side by side as the sun climbed to the top of the hay rack, and beyond,

we worked and sweated, swinging arms in that ancient rhythm,
bringing in the harvest. I did not know I could be so strong;
I surprised us both, matching you bale for bale. We did not talk,
saving our energy for the endless field before us. Sun and dust,

horseflies and gnats, ice water and sweat, the small relief of sitting
while you drove to the next row. That was our world that day.
We loaded the rack to the top, then climbed into the truck for home.
I think I slept. Too soon, the aching work began in reverse:

to load the hay bales into the barn loft. I almost cried then, but settled
once more into the work that must be done: catch, turn,
stack, turn to catch again. No thought of work's ending and rest beyond;
only the work itself existed. Staggering home in firefly darkness,

I knew I had visited only for a day the bone-deep work of your life,
and felt pride to have shared it. In the moments before exhaustion won,
I heard you say, "She worked like a man," and smiled. You meant well.
And next morning: "I'm proud of you."

Into whatever darkness has come, that day
has blazed its light; whenever soul's winter came bellowing
hunger, that day has fed me with its truth: be strong,
keep your head down, keep working, there is more to be done,

do it and be done. I have done no finer work
than that day hauling hay with you.

## Two-Dog Night (Insomnia)

From my side of the bed, certain sounds freeze
me into stillness: the turning tick of
fan blades; the happy sigh of your good dog
who sleeps in simple, silent faithfulness;
and through the floor beneath, where Annie cries,
confined to kennel and to cage, the click
of nails against her prison wall, the moan
and whine of sorrow, or regret.  Some sounds,
and yet their absence too, can lock me in:
stale air unstirred—breath too long unreleased—
the silence when I turn to you.  Like her,
I cannot move beyond this wall.  She yearns
for hands to open, voice to beckon her
to warmth and welcome on the other side.

## Relinquishment

Each night the softly-closing bedroom door
sets my bounds—*here*—and nevermore the right
to find our bed, the haven of your arms;
too long, too cold the years of sleepless nights
to be reclaimed.  I am all emptiness.
Breast and nape and thigh, each knows this sadness:
no one now aches for them.  The lips they knew
will never seek them out in slow dark sips.
I lean my cheek upon the door between;
your dreaming sigh drifts faintly through the oak.
Its surface dares me, a blank page on which
my hope—my shame—is drawn in nightly strokes.
Dare I break the page, dare write the story new?
—I turn away, and leave the dreams to you.

The resurrection, when it comes, will not blaze forth
in glory-light, all halo and wing
and shouting trumpets; nor will it arrive, agreed-upon,
with the clashed swords of long debate,
souls wrestling with words until darkness yields to dawn
and stone rolls away on cue.

Instead, you will stand in your kitchen, stock-still,
as though listening intently to the night—
raucous katydids, and spring peepers, and the one bullfrog
who rules the goldfish pond—
you will absently run a butter knife through the spilled biscuit
flour on the countertop,

waiting, waiting for your carefully-scripted moment.
Not then will it come, not when
the space between you shrinks to an aching ragged breath;
not when the lamp clicks off
and the bedroom door clicks shut
for the thousandth time between you, when something brittle

and bruised inside you finally breaks;
nor when the animal cry wells up from some deep place,
twisting face and body until you are bent,
there in your kitchen, into a silent screaming prayer.
Lost. Lost. Lost. No maps for these dark roads;
gripping this wheel breaks and crazes every nail.

This prayer will pass through you like a fire;
and through the blowing ash that remains,
a whisper of a voice long-forgotten, heavy and warm
as a quilt stitched by every mother
you have known: *Peace, child. Go lay thee down.*
*The body knows best the heart of us.*

And as you turn the knob of a door that has been shut
a thousand times, you will hear it again:
the maddening siren of the cicadas, the yearning call
of every animal body; and you will step through
a door, a wall; a fear: a fall. Only then will it come,
that first new breath. You will breathe it together.

**Yalad**

No hand-maiden I, husband; not for me
to bear his cup. Instead, I was to be
the obedient cup itself, brim-full
with strange wine: water and blood: holiness.

The sacrifices smolder still, the moon
returns, my time complete; and I remain
unknown to you. Too long have we been twined
about with shadows: let us be done with holy things.

Here I lay aside all mystery—turn, a simple girl
to arms that carried me, hands that caught the child,
wrapped him tenderly, as tenderly bound my wound—
your trembling hands now the only blessedness I seek.

The angel's words to me I now proclaim to you: Fear not!
something new awaits its birth. Take up this cup—deeply drink.


(*Yalad*, from the Hebrew, meaning "to be born")

**The Root Defiant**
    *(for Katy)*


The gardener toils and, splicing strength to strength,
engrafts the sturdy root of apple tree
to graceful weeping crab. The grafted tree
is planted; grows as planned; but in its shade

another grows: a girl, apple-blossomed hair
and feet bird-swift; laughter brimming, spilling,
until the years of darkness slow their flight,
dam up the stream and dim her radiant hair.

O Tree-girl. O Girl-tree. In the silence
of your roots is held the truth of who you are.
Go there. Listen. Embrace and be embraced.
No time remains for this trailing habit:

See the long-diminished root express
its branching hunger for the light,
declare in greenest strength, *I will no longer weep, but stand.*

# River Prayers

## I
## Eden, Imagined

Stand with me. Cupped hands held before you: this long valley.
Breathe gently, just so: rolling clouds, morning fog.

With silent house behind you holding its breath, imagine:
divine breath sweeping back the mist of centuries, revealing this land

as it lay, unbound by roads or cables, innocent of buildings,
engines, factories, unmapped save by the feet of those
who walked its intimate paths, knew its nameless hills.


Now further back. Hands, palms to sky:
imagine this valley no valley at all,
this hawk-stitched ridge the sunless floor of a quiet inland sea,

familiar green stories of dogwood and trillium, acorn and hickory
not yet written on the folded land. Troubled spine of limestone
waits for its moment of upthrust and heave, creatures of shell and salt

hover, patient, for the glacial movement
of water's perfect truth to find its way, make a road
for sea to become river, wear the mountain down.


Can you hear the questions that breathe out
from these stones, these woods and waters?

What shattering raised the stony crest now shielding your softest heart?
How many tears, and whose, flow in that river sweetly bearing away,
grit by bitterest grit, the ache that even now grinds itself in your bones?

What new paths will open in your heart when that holy joy,
laughing, sweeps away the fears that tangle there?  What hand
will invite you into what green dance,
across what white-blooming field?


## II
**All Things Rise**

River and shore lay swathed still in their bedclothes:
mist and cloud fine-woven by some skilled Hand.

All is quiet, and so am I.

I will content myself to listen, here at morningside,
for the sun's gentle matins:

the squirrel who emerges from nest high above
and chatters his prayers down the tree-way;

late-to-bed owl who haunts some rabbit's dreams
with her low thrumming wings and eternal question;

a beaver, river-sleek, who slaps and bubbles, then flows as silk,
seeming but a darker current in the ridge-shadowed water.

If I remain still, mountain and water and sky
will allow me to stand witness to these sacred moments.

If I remain still, perhaps you—
O my brother and O my sister—
will allow me to stand witness to yours.

The sun lifts with its rising
the cover of mist and cloud
the wing of owl and heron
the voice of squirrel and robin and jay
the heart of turtle and fish
and this night-chilled heart of mine.

I rise, too, and stand beside you—
O my brother and O my sister—
to join the day.


**III**

**To Know a River**
*(for a 30th anniversary)*

To know a river like an old friend—

    that this spot is too shallow even for your nimble kayak,
    that there in the quiet hallow behind that island,
    the heron build their nests,
    that here the current confuses itself
    around blind submerged rocks
    and will tear the paddle from your hands—

To know a river for these long years is not to say
that it cannot, even now, surprise you—

    that the comic flap and dive of the curmudgeonly turtle
    will no longer make you laugh out loud;
    that the startle of wing and fin
    cannot race your heart;

that the benison of the eagle's cry
no longer sings itself in your blood;

that the sudden fountain of butterflies clustering on the shore
cannot still the engine of thought
nor draw you into that quivering congregation of antennae and wing
murmuring to itself in all its silent ways: "Oh, you are beautiful;
tell me I am beautiful, too."

To live with a river is to understand
that it changes and surprises
even as you live your daily tedium,
happy or discontented, on its nearer shore.

How long does it take, I wonder,
to say that you know a river?
Thirty years and more, I suppose,
is not too long to know and yet still be surprised,
to know that the bleaching whale-bone of the fallen sycamore
does not sing the whole story, the full history of storm and flood,
the torn-root damage that we sorrow over but cannot heal.

Not too long to hope again for that trembling moment,
like the delicate touch of wing:
Oh love, you are beautiful; tell me I am beautiful, too.

## IV
**Messenger**

Three crows, flying low across my path.  Once, walking south in twilight along the river's edge; twice, driving north in morning sun.  Same river.  Same road.  Same crows.  Same sun gleaming blackwing.

What augur do they bring?  The mountains tell us: illness in the house?  Rain, or the unexpected guest?   That guest most unwanted,
except when—at the end of all pain—
death appears, heaven's most welcomed kindness?

Or perhaps, just this: the bright lift of wings into air,
canes arching over the path,
berry's darkling tumble into my palm,
summer sun burst ecstatic on my tongue?
If I may choose between messengers, my heart says *yes*:
let this sweetness in at the door.

**Lessons in Ballad-Singing**


All that your teachers have taught you before: unlearn.
Come to this singing green, fresh, newly-minted;
or else tired, broken. Surrendered. Either will serve.


*First, the breath.* Deep, if you can. Steep trails leave little
to the lungs for singing. Stay a while, rest here. When you are ready,
sigh. Let the phrase catch, let the highest tones hitch and weep.
Let the breath sift low through chinks, strained wild
by tangled bittersweet. The higher, the harder. Trust:
what makes it through will be enough.


*Next, the palate.* Few cathedrals and vaulted spaces here;
our openness is a more homely kind. Use the spaces most familiar:
dim overgrown path, narrow gap of ridge-bound sky;
low mineral roof burrowed into black rock. Vowels twist and flatten,
shorten to conform. We sing the way we dream.


*Finally, the lips and teeth.* Held quiet and close, they should not
emote or draw attention. Grit them against the song,
against pain, against the force of breath. This sets a fine edge.


*And now, the final alchemy,* the gold no one has yet mined:
sing a place for yourself into even the oldest song—
this the sweetest room that is yours alone.

**Understory**
*(Red in the Bud)*


This is our time, declare the small quiet ones.

While those known for grand gestures clutch to themselves
their demure greens, their virginal white wraps,
their thickest robes of clouded bloom to veil late-winter nakedness,

we stand and declare our lines in fire –
line them out clearly, so that you might sing them too,
might trace each knot, each broken place—

might see last summer's heat run along the limb,
clinging like silk, draping each branch with the desire
of winter's long-pent waiting.

This is our time.  We know that soon enough,
we will again take our place in the understory,
unseen, unmarked in the green season.

This brief moment when we sing our story,
*brightflame* licking along the bones:
it is all we are, all we have to tell.
A poet her words.  A singer his song.

Tracy wasn't born in West Virginia, but as the saying goes, she got there as soon as she could. The path to her West By God Virginia homeplace wandered through Texas, Arkansas, Florida, (then) West Germany, California, and Virginia. During her half-a-lifetime of wandering, she earned a bachelor's and a master's degree, both in English, from Lyon College (formerly Arkansas College) in Batesville, Arkansas; and from The College of William and Mary in Virginia in Williamsburg. She currently serves as registrar for Shepherd University, a public liberal arts university in Shepherdstown, West Virginia, where she also coordinates a local chapter of the national non-profit, Team River Runner, serving veterans in recovery from combat by teaching them recreational, therapeutic, and adaptive kayaking.

All of her homes have been near rivers or other flowing water: the Lampasas, the Spring, the Hillsborough and the Gulf of Mexico, the White, the Main, and now the Potomac and the Shenandoah. She now lives with her family on the banks of the Shenandoah River, under the shadow of the Blue Ridge.

Though her study of poetry was deep and delicious, she did not begin writing her own poetry until she moved to her West Virginia riverside home, in 2003. She is grateful for the small, steady stream of positive responses to her work through the West Virginia Writers community and through various regional literary journals, both print and online, including *Bluestone Review, Backbone Mountain Review, Pine Mountain Sand & Gravel Literary Journal, the Anthology of Appalachian Writers,* and in online journals including *Still: The Journal* and *Assisi: an Online Journal of Arts and Letters.* Her 2013 participation in the Appalachian Writer's Workshop at the Hindman Settlement School in Kentucky was an important catalyst for many of the works in this volume.

She is grateful beyond measure to her teachers, mentors, and encouragers across the miles and years: to Drs. Terrell Tebbetts and Charles Oliver* of Lyon College; to F. Ethan Fischer* and Dr. Sylvia Shurbutt of Shepherd University; to her companions and teachers at the AWW-Hindman program; and of course to her husband George, whose quiet encouragement for over 30 years has been both an open door to exploration, and a deep welcome back home.

*deceased

www.ingramcontent.com/pod-product-compliance
Lightning Source LLC
LaVergne TN
LVHW041513070426
835507LV00012B/1540